Here is a collection of funny letters, silly blunders and comical howlers - clangers dropped by Headteachers, Teachers and children all over the country. Misprints and malapropisms and the funny things that children say, all with witty drawings that capture the flavour of **The Funny Side of School.**

IF YOU NEED A
MISTRESS
URGENTLY
IN THE NIGHT
RING THE BELL

THE FUNNY SIDE

OF

SCHOOL

Roy Shipperbottom
and
Carolyn W. Webster

Illustrated by Henry Brewis

Nutmeg Press

Nutmeg Press, 9 Southgate,
Heaton Chapel, Stockport SK4 4QL

© Roy Shipperbottom and Carolyn W. Webster 1985
© Illustrations Henry Brewis 1985

ISBN 0 946816 02 6

Typeset by Tech-Set, Gateshead, Tyne and Wear
and printed by Richard Clay plc, Bungay, Suffolk.

ACKNOWLEDGEMENTS

We are grateful to all the following teachers and lecturers, working and retired who told or wrote about incidents at school. We are particularly thankful for the contributions of Maud Rand, who at the age of 99 wrote two long letters packed with howlers, Ray Russell of Dersingham, Kings Lynn for pages of incidents in his life as a Headmaster and Marjorie Styan of Stockton on Tees who opened up a rich seam of History Howlers.

Percy Abbott
Bill Bagley
S. J. Beattie
Wendy Betts
Pam Bowes
Joe Burke
Jean Clarkson
W. S. Close
Joan Cohan
H. S. Cousins
Harvey Dearden
Aileen Deare
Tom and Leonie Dunk
Maud Farrington
W. G. Franklin
June Greenbank
Joan Hancock
Doreen Handy
Frank A. Harris
W. Hudson
Jack Kelly
Wilf Kenworthy
Mrs E. M. King
Joan Knight
Miss Lawson

Miss Lawton
A. J. Lock
Margaret Mayne
Mary Y. Mutch
Derek Penna
Kathy Percival
Maud Rand
Ray Russell
Doreen Scott
V. Silkstone
Sheila Smith
Susan Smith
Barry Rea
Brian Rose
Ian Swanney
Peter Stainton
Judy Taylor
Peter Taylor
Allan D. Temple
Carol Thompson
Vivian Webb
Vivienne Welsh
Oliver Whyman
John Whitworth

We are indebted to hundreds of children, all over the country, who have unknowingly contributed and also those who remembered the daft things teachers sometimes say.

We are always pleased to see new material about 'The Funny Side of School' and welcome any contributions which will be acknowledged in the next book which is now in preparation.
Please send all material to:
Carolyn W. Webster,
72 Hanover Drive,
Winlaton
BLAYDON
Tyne and Wear NE21 6BA

INTRODUCTION

Teachers were collecting Howlers a hundred years ago and Mark Twain, in the Century magazine for April 1887 wrote:

'I have just fallen upon a darling literary curiosity . . . a collection made by a teacher and all the examples are genuine, none of them have been tampered with or doctored in any way. From time to time, during several years, whenever a pupil has delivered himself of anything peculiarly quaint or toothsome in the course of his recitations, this teacher and her associates have privately set that thing down.'

Even then seventeen of the examples he quoted from 'English as She is Taught' published in the United States had also appeared in an English magazine a year earlier.

We know that some contributions to The Funny Side of School are from vintage years and have labelled them as classics. Some contributors sent photocopies of mistakes and there is no doubt that if you ask young children to draw 'The Flight into Egypt' they will portray the Holy Family in an aeroplane. We can believe that at some time a child may have labelled the pilot 'Pontius' and the variations on this one theme could occupy a page. Phonetic spelling will render wrapped as raped and the unassisted child will produce his own version of 'pennies'.

Sometimes daft answers are the result of daft questions and we have brought together the things some teachers say and these have been remembered, sometimes many years later, with affection. Just as Oliver Goldsmith in The Deserted Village wrote of the schoolmaster and the children

Full well they laughted with counterfeited glee
At all his Jokes, for many a joke had he.

Or that old boys of one famous school remembered their headmasters advice

'Boys, let the coruscations of your wit be like the scintillations of summer lightning — lambent yet innocuous.'

Now, as we go to print there comes news that Nunthorpe Grammar School, York ordered 1000 specially designed mugs to commemorate the closure of the school. They arrived with the word 'Grammar' misspelt as 'Grammer'. One pupil said that, 'The mistake was announced at assembly and everybody laughed — even the teachers seemed to see the funny side.'

ABSENTEE NOTES

I am very sorry but . . .
Mary was away from school because she had the windy spasms.

I gave my son a half-holiday.

Peter had tooth ache all over.

Jean has been very ill under the treatment of the doctor.

He has had whopping cough.

He is having trouble with his lover.

9

We kept her off to help as her granny has a cute angina.

Please excuse Lizzie as she couldn't stand on her feet with her head.

CLASSIC COLLECTION

Mary can't come to school this morning because she hasn't been. I've given her something and if she goes I'll see that she comes.

John has panes in his head and his nose is steaming with a cold.

* * *

Janet has been a little sack.

The doctor has tasted his urine and has sent a sample to the hospital so it can be tasted there.

I am sorry Jean was away with pans in her head and pans in her back which she has had for a long time.

Tony fell in the river and had to be given the kiss of death.

We kept Barbara away because her grandmother died to oblige her mother.

David has a sore stomach and we want to see what comes out of it.

Harry has a gumboil on the back of his thigh.

We are very worried about Janet's heart and I am sorry to have to tell you it is still beating.

I was afraid that his finger was going sceptic.

His face has broken out in a rush through his inside.

To the Head Waster, Sir Barry has cut his thumb.

Peter has been hit on the head by a heavy football.It has left him with a bad head which I hope he shakes off.

CLASSIC COLLECTION

I am sorry but . . .

She is under the Doctor and he doesn't seem to be doing her any good.

Wayne had diarrhoea through a hole in his shoe giving him a chill.

Bill's father died and had to be buried and Tom had to help.

* * *

Dear Miss,

Please excuse Natalie not coming to school yesterday afternoon as she had the baby while I went to the hospital.

Yours truly,

Mrs. K. D.

Dear Teacher,

Tommy could not come with his stomach.

Jane is under the doctor again.

Michael has an illustrated throat.

She has contacted sore eyes.

She has headaches again and it seems that this is her weak part.

The baby has a rush and it might be catching.

RECEPTION CLASS

A teacher saw the five year old boy hobble into the Hall with great difficulty and discovered that he had been told to change his shoes for P.E. and had put his on opposite feet.
"David, you have your shoes on the wrong feet"
"Oh Miss these are the only feet I've got."

The caretaker, Mr. Rollinson, brought his homing pigeon to school. The children enjoyed his talk and asked all kinds of questions about pigeons and really did enjoy the experience. I was on playground duty when the caretaker came into the yard and made a great show about sending the bird home to tell his wife to get his tea ready. One of the reception class asked me what was going on. I carefully explained that the pigeon was flying to Mr. Rollinson's house. The child looked earnestly at the sky at the fast disappearing pigeon and turned to me and said, "Does Mr. Rollinson live with Jesus then? I didn't know that."

"Please Miss. Can I have some water for my consecrated orange juice?"

CLASSIC

The sentence said by hundreds of women teachers to men visiting schools or at social functions when the phrase always seems to find one of those silences which ensures that everyone hears it.
   "Are you the father of one of my children?"

Childrens sayings — After the first day at school

"Poor mother. I know now that you don't know anything."

"Mummy, that teacher didn't know how to spell CAT and I had to tell her."

"The teacher said that I have to go back again tomorrow."

"Daddy, I told the teacher that I am an only child and absolutely ruined by my mother and granny who give me too much money. But I am saving up to buy things like a nightie for mummy and pyjamas for you then you will have something to wear in bed."

Teacher: Stop sniffing, David have you no handkerchief?
David: Yes Miss but I can't lend it to you.

Parent to Reception Class teacher:

"You always take the reception class Mrs. Webster. Never mind perhaps one day they will let you take an older class."

Father: "Well, Thomas, what did you learn on your first day at school?"

Thomas: "I learned that other boys get pocket money from their daddy every Friday."

MIXED INFANTS

A 6 year old approached the teacher with her spelling book and said, "Please, how do you spell sex?"
Teacher: "Are you sure that's the word you want?"
"Yes – I've written 'in' – I want 'sex' " (insects)

Jim, a supply teacher was asked to take the Nursery for a few days, in a school completely staffed by women. The children had quite a lot of difficulty in adjusting to a male teacher and after a few days he suggested that they should call him Uncle rather than "Miss". The following day was hot and the shallow pool in the playground was full of naked nursery children. After some time a little lad went up to Jim and shly asked "Uncle, if you take your clothes off will you be a man or a lady?"

Teacher, to a six year old,
        "Can you write yet Margaret?"
Margaret: "Yes, but not that scribble sort of writing you do on the board."

Teacher, Reading to infants . . . and the frog was very ugly . . . can you tell me a word that means "not ugly"?
Child, enthusiastically, "Posh!"

An infant asked the dinner lady, "Please is it safe to eat trifle with a soup spoon?"

THE JUNIORS

I read a poem to a class of seven year old children about a granny who knitted clothes for animals and birds. She knitted an eight fingered mitten for an octopus. I asked the children why she would knit an eight fingered mitten. Only one hand went up.
"Yes?"
"Well Miss an octopus has eight testicles."

Ann came up to the teacher and said, "My Aunt has had a miniature baby – it only weighs four pounds". She gave daily reports on the progress of the premature baby and one day burst into the room and said, "The miniature baby is going to leave hospital." The headmistress was present and asked how heavy the baby was.
"Five pounds, Miss."
"That is a tiny baby."
"Yes Miss, but they have only been married five months."

"They live in caravans and travel from place to place and so it is difficult for them to get regular lessons," said Mrs. Hope who specialises in teaching tipsy children.

"Last year they stopped using little birds down coal mines. These birds were used to find out if there were dangerous gases.
Does anyone know the type of bird that was used?"
"I do Miss – a mynah bird!"

The miners are all given lambs before they go underground.

The money they use in Greece is called draculas.

16

Little boy (crying): "I don't like school and I have just been told I have to stay till I'm 16."

Teacher: "Never mind – I have to stay till I'm 60."

Heard in the Staffroom.

One thing that's better teaching here in a Primary School – there's always room to park a car.

PRIMARY GRAFFITTI

Now I lay me down to rest,
I pray to pass tomorrows test
If I should die before I wake,
That's one less test I have to take.

Roses are red, Violets are blue,
I copied your homework,
I failed too.

God made the bees and they make honey,
We do the work and teachers make the money.

An inspector came into out class and he knew nothing so he asked
us and we had to tell him.

From a story written by a Junior.

The little boys and girls stood with their faces pressed to the shop
widow.

A bungalow is a house with the upstairs downstairs.

The power of advertising

The Remedial Reading Group were doing letter "A" and the teacher
asked for words beginning with an "A" sound and showed the class
pictures including an apple.

"What sound does that begin with?"

"Cr" said Alan, "Cr."

"Why do you say 'Cr' Alan?"

"Cr for crunch Miss."

Teacher: "Suppose I gave you these two apples, a large shiny red one and this old green one and asked you to share them with your brother. Which one would you keep – the red one?"

Harry: "Which brother – my little brother or my big one?"

Teacher: Jason! why are you chasing Jennifer?

Jason: Because she pinched me.

Teacher: Why did you pinch him Jennifer?

Jennifer: So that he'd chase me Miss.

Notes passed in class.

Dear Jane,

    I love you.

      Love

       David

The reply

Dear David,

    I don't love you,

      Love,

       Jane

A 5 year old describes his bald headmaster.

"His head is coming out of his hair."

NATURE STUDY

The cuckoo is a very lazy bird, it doesn't even lay it's own eggs.

A cuckoo lays other birds eggs in its own nest and vice versa.

Teacher: "Isn't it amazing how the chicks break out of the shells?"

Infant: "I think it's amazing how they get in."

The animal I would most like to see is a dinosaur but they have all gone. They used to roam the earth before the world was ever made.

Farmer's Son: "Miss we've got a pigeon in our barn."

Teacher: "Really Paul – is it a wood pigeon?"

Paul: "No! It's a live one."

Odd Spellings

egog (hedgehog)

The rabbit was behind yrntn (wire netting)

ASSEMBLY

A diminutive headmaster used to conduct Assembly in the schoolyard. He stood on a chair to see the boys in their lines and said

"Our Father, don't shuffle, which art, get in line, get in line boy, in heaven. Hallowed be thy name, thy – you are late Jackson stop smiling and take your cap off . . . I know we are outside but we are at prayer aren't we Clegg? See me after, Thy Kingdom wasn't it . . . anyway it doesn't matter because its beginning to rain . . . everybody inside."

Primary School versions of the Lord's Prayer

Our Father, we charge in Heaven

Our Father and Mark and Kevin

Our Father which art in Devon

Thy King cum cum

Harold be thy name

Hello be thy name

Lead us not into Thames Station

'This morning let us pray that the trouble between the Arabs and the Israelis can be settled in a true Christian manner.

Hymns

Holy, Holy, Holy, Merciful and Mighty,
God with free Persil, Blessed Trinity.

My favourite hymn is the one about carrots of fire.

* * *

CLASSIC

"Mother I'm not going to school this morning."

"Why not?"

"The boys don't like me and the staff don't like me."

"Son you are going to school, you're forty five years old and you're the Headmaster"

THE HEAD SPEAKS

A parent once said to me that half the teachers here did all the work and the other half did nothing – I can assure you that the reverse is the case.

A Junior comments on the Headmaster.

Our Headmaster does not swear but when he is upset he says, "God bless my sole."

Headmaster!   "James, why do you answer me by asking another question?"

James: "Do I Sir?"

Teacher in a convent school run by a religious order
"Girls you must never, never sit with your legs crossed. You have
never seen a photograph of Our Lady, the Holy Mother sitting
with her legs crossed and you never will."

"I have had Miss Jones on the carpet in my room but failed to get
any satisfaction."

"This behaviour is disgraceful and must never happen again. If
the founder of this school were alive today he would be turning
in his grave."

*An entry in a school punishment book by a Headmistress who had,
without entering the outside lavatories, observed the behaviour of
two boys.*

Punishment: 3 strokes of the cane.
Reason: Urinating to competitive altitudes.

From a letter a Headmaster wrote about a idle lad whose father was Chairman of Governors.

"If you can get him to work for you, you will be most fortunate."

Sign on photocopier
Reproduction equipment is not for playing with and must not be used without my permission

Extract from MEMO
It is necessary to compile a return of teachers broken down by sex, qualifications and age.

"Is it true you are leaving us?"
"Yes Headmaster – after fifteen years."
"Pity, I was just getting used to you."

I want to know if anything is going seriously wrong; then I can help. But don't come to me to save your bacon when the baby has gone down the plughole or been thrown away with the bathwater.

If I was asked to sum up, in one word, the qualities of the staff of this school it would be "Team Spirit".

"It may be that at some time you will feel you cannot go on; maybe there is an examination you cannot face, and life is difficult and then you will turn to God or you can come and see me."

ST. GABRIEL
GETS NEW HEAD

Lord dismiss us.
"To those who are leaving us today I will say that as you go out into the world you may come face to face with those who are losing their heads . . ."

THE THINGS TEACHERS SAY

Now girls I want you to watch the blackboard while I go through it.

MEMO:

To: The Headmaster, Ward B3

From: The Staff

We understand that the operation was successful and thought that you would like to know that at a staff meeting today it was resolved to wish you a speedy recovery by 31 votes to 9.

Staffroom Comments

"I'll say this for the new Headmaster he's nasty but fair." "What do you mean- fair?"
"I mean that he's nasty to everybody."

"If the intellect in this room was equivalent to string there wouldn't be enough to tie round a midget's toe."

"Whatever time she can spare from combing her hair or applying make-up she spends neglecting her work."

EXTRACTS FROM MEMOS

TO: HEADMASTER
FROM: SCHOOL COUNSELLING SERVICE

. . . they have a lodger who stays in at night and is responsible for the children . . . but the home is breaking up – the relatives are helping.

The mother has been in a car crash and speaks broken English.

Now that the father has gone back to work on a tanker her mother is able to handle her affairs much better.

I have received the enclosed note from Susan's mother,

Dear Mrs. Williams,

Please understand me when I say that I know you mean well telling our Susan about her pregnancy but please leave these matter for the doctor who is responsible for her condition.

Yours sincerely.

Teachers reports on accidents and incidents

I took Vicky to the Accident Department at the Hospital for treatment and I am pleased that she left there with no bones broken.

The fire in the pavilion was extinguished before much damage was done by the local fire brigade.

Extracts from references written for colleagues

Miss Warlock, who is certified, has also taken an Open University degree.

Mr. Baker is a popular member of staff who handles young girls superbly.

He is a sound candidate for the position he seeks:
he has good judgement; he is not married.

Job Interviews

The Chairman of Governors starts the meeting.

"The five young ladies who have been shortlisted are waiting in the corridor. I don't think I have ever seen five more expectant women."

Residential malajusted art teacher required to start in September.

LETTERS FROM PARENTS

Dear Teacher,

I know Jacqueline has had some time off with her bowels and I think this was because she was worried about her music examination. She is now better and you will be glad to know that she has passed the piano.

Yours truly,

Dear Teacher,

Wayne came home very upset because you said he was illiterate. The fact is that his mother and me were married in June and he was born in August so you see that he is no more illiterate than you or me.

Thank you.
Waynes Father.

Dear Teacher,

I have read Mark's report and the results are terrible. Why don't you get off your fat backside and not be so idle and do what you are paid to do – Teach!

Please excuse pencil,
Yours very truly,

Dear Teacher,

I have seen in the paper that you want to know if you can punish children. You can punish mine as I am in favour of discipline and capital punishment for children as it never did me any harm.

Thank you.

PARENTS VISIT THE SCHOOL

> The Parent Teachers made the Hall most attractive with decorative pants.

The classroom door was flung open and there stood Bill's father complaining that the teacher had thumped little Bill. The teacher said that all the details were in the staffroom and he would fetch them and asked Bill's father to "Keep this lot quiet until I get back." He went to the staffroom for the punishment book, made a cup of tea, lit a cigarette, drank the tea and waited for the sound to grow in volume as the class began to erupt. At the critical time the teacher moved back down the corridor to be met by Bill's father shouting, "Here, mate, thump the bloody lot!"

At the Parents Evening
"I'm Terry Jackson's father. What do you teach?"
"Physical Science"
"Ah yes – all that running and jumping."

Teacher: "John still has trouble with some of his sounds when he's talking. Do you still take him to the Speech Therapist?"

Parent: "No, I don't take him any more. They didn't do no good – the women just used to talk to him."

Teacher: "Hello Mrs. Harrison – I see your husband's not with you this evening."

Mrs Harrison: "No he's very tired. He had an accident to his head and during the night I was so frightened that I had to wake him up every five minutes to see if he was dead."

Malaprop Corner
"Thank you, Headmaster, you're a mind of information"

PARENTS

"Hello, Mrs. Jackson, how's your little girl?"
"Not so little – she took her entrance test for the grammar school last week and she didn't pass. The terrible thing is that if she had been born a day later she could have taken it again next year."

"Oh what a pity and it's just what you don't think about at the time."

PARENT TEACHERS JUMBLE SALE

Bring something you don't need
Bring your Wives and Husbands

A Yorkshire schoolmistress was asked to sign a form to enable a parent to get an allowance. The mother said "You know if you were paid for every one of these forms you sign you would make quite a bit of money."

"Oh yes," said the teacher," I know a doctor who charges two pounds for signing them."

"Ah yes but then the doctor's time is valuable." replied the mother.

Bloom Street Primary P.T.A.
are holding a social evening
on Wednesday 5th June.
The Junior Choir will sin.

MATHS

The answer is 38.86997632547297593 approximately.

A polygon has many sides, an octogan eight but we have not been told about hooligans.

If you curve a straight line right round so that it comes back you have a circle if you put a dot in the middle.

Question: What is half of nine?

Answer: There is a big half and a little half. The big half is five and the little half if four.

Teacher to young mother with four children

"Hello, Barbara, I see you finally learned to multiply."

REPORTS

MATHEMATICS 8% There is one consolation-with these low marks he cannot be cheating.

ARITHMETIC   Alan's inability at arithmetic is disgraceful for both of us – I however do try.

Mother: "Hello Milly, how did you go on at school today?

Milly: "I got a gold star in arithmetic"

Mother: "Wonderful; What's three and two?"

Milly: "We haven't done that yet."

A few months later . . .
Mother: "Milly, what's thirteen times four?"

Milly: "There's no thirteen times anything."

Things which are equal to each other are equal to anything else.

Teacher: "What would you rather have eight sixteenths of an orange or half an orange?"

Boy: "Half an orange, Sir."

Teacher: "It would be the same wouldn't it?"

Boy: "No Sir, you would lose a lot of juice cutting it up into sixteenths."

An angle is like a triangle but without one side.

Teacher: "If you have a piece of meat and divide it into two you will have two halves. Now divide each half again and think what you have. Now divide again and once more. What have you now?"

Boy: "Mince."

A polygon is a square with a lot of sides.

Father: "Shall I help you with your homework sums Janet?"

Janet: "No I shall only get into trouble tomorrow if they are right."

ENGLISH

My father says that the rats are too high and should come down.

When Prince Charles came the police put up barristers but Prince Charles came up to the barristers and shook hands over the barristers with all the old ladies.

The children wandered through the Highlands of Scotland and saw the famous Highland cattle. I do not know if the cattle took their name from the Highlands or the Highlands took their name from the cattle.

I have decided not to go to college but to stay on at school and continue my education.

A gentleman is a man who gives up his seat to a lady in a public convenience.

If I had a flat of my own I would brighten it up by putting the paint on myself.

The School Horticultural Society welcomed Mr. Bolton who talked on the subject "Pests in the Garden". There were a large number present.

Aunts in the garden are a pest and must be got rid of.

When they went round the side of the rocks all of a sudden an awful abbess yawned in front of them.

Bakers put yeast into their loves to make them rise.

Edgar Allen Poe is a very curdling writer.

Chaucer was the father of English pottery.
Chaucer was a bland verse writer of the third century.

Homers writings include Paradise Lost and Homer's Essays which some people say were not written by Homer but by another man of the same name.

A man called Bowdler cut the dirty bits out of Shakespeare. When Shakespeare wrote "Go to" Bowdler cut the next word out and that is why it reads strange.

Write three or four sentences to describe a policeman, a postman, a railway guard and a fireman.

A policeman is a man who goes round at night to see if the widows are fast.

Coleridge was on drugs and wrote a poem which began;
In Xanadu did Klu Klux Klan a stately pleasure dome and then
forgot the rest.

A teacher introduces Shakespeare.

In these lessons we will be coming across words that might make
some of you snigger. Words that are earthy, bawdy-four letter
words. One four letter word you will have to get used to is w-o-r-k.

In "The Tempest" one of the main characters is Prospero who
has a daughter called Veranda.

Some poems are written in heroic cutlets

Hamlet is one of the set plays for the examination and we presen-
ted scenes from the play for the parents on Open Day. No doubt
some of them had seen it before but they laughed all the
same.

An example of the Romantic Movement was Romeo and
Juliet.

HISTORY

They bought goods at retail prices and sold them at wholesale prices. This made things a lot easier for the customers.

The canals of England were dug by knaves. Knaves are very strong men who now only dig up roads.

The kings stoutest supporters were the fat ones.

St. Pauls Cathedral was designed by Christoper Robin.

Bonnie Prince Charlie flew from Scotland to France.

The nights finished off Thomas Becket.

Queen Victoria was the longest queen. She sat on the thorn for more than sixty years.

Lord Nelson died from being mortally killed at Waterloo which is why we have Trafalgar Square not far from Charing Cross.

King Harold mustarded his men before the Battle of Hastings.

Magna Carta said that no man should be hanged twice for the same offence.

Columbus was always cursing about the Atlantic.

COLLECTED CLASSICS:

Drake circumcised the world with a forty foot cutter. When they told him that they had seen the invisible Armada he was playing a game and said that the Amarda could wait but his bowels couldn't. Queen Elizabeth knitted him on the deck of his ship for singing the beard of the King of Spain.

A history teacher, who gives such entertaining lessons that even tough truants attend regularly, is reputed to end her lessons like this, "Will Napoleon manage to get back to France? If he does will he get men to follow him? How will England's Iron Duke react? Be here, next week, same time, same place, to find out what happens next!"

Nigel, who has been in hospital for some time, returns to school.

History Teacher; "Nigel you are really going to have to work hard to make up for lost time. How long have you been away?"

Nigel; "Since the Crimean War Sir."

King Henry VIII thought so much of Wolsey that he made him a cardigan.

Cromwell had a large wart on his nose but underneath there were deep religious feelings.

Then there were three more crusades – each of which came after the one before.

After he had killed King Harold the new King was William the Conjuror.

The Romans made their roads straight so that the Britons could not hide round the corners.

In the olden days they built some nice things but also many ruins.

Abraham Lincoln was born in a log cabin he built himself.

Disraeli bought the shares of the sewage canal and laid them at the feet of his adoring young Queen.

Mary Queen of Scots was well known and lots of people knew her because she was well known and when I say she was well known I mean well known.

The Civil War was a bad war and many people died a lot and you can't do nowt about it now.

Mother's comments on Report

"I know his History marks are very low but it was a very unfair examination. They asked him about things that happened before he was even born."

At Pompeii 2,000 people were trapped and dyed. The only eye witness of this was Pluto. The whole city was covered with boiling larva.

The three vows taken by a monk are chastity, poverty and humidity.

A mummy was not a Mummy and Daddy mummy. It is a name given to dead people raped in bandages. Egyptians used to mummy dead bodies before burying themselves.

Trade began in the Bronze Age because every body started to want bronze and exchanged the traders for it.

CLASSIC COLLECTION

Joan of Arc was a pheasant when she was fifteen she made friends with a French soldier and put spirit into him. Later she walked into the middle of a crowd and picked out the King himself. Alright said the King I give up. He took the girl into his room and she told him what she had come for. Joan was burned at the steak but next day they found her heart as good as new.

Richard III lost his throne at Bosworth, but one of Henry VII's followers picked it up and put it on his head.

Louis XVI married Marianne Toinette.

The clergy in France were all Catholic. They were also split down the middle before the revolution.

The Burglars of Calais had to be beheaded, belegged, bearmed and their head tied together.

Factory owners soon stopped this reduction in adults hours by putting the children into shifts.

At a Roman circus they sent about a hundred people into a stadium and let the lions loos onto them.

Fill in the missing words:

a. Between 1536 and 1540 King Henry VIII dissolved the _____ aspirin

b. The supporters of Charles 1 in the civil war were called _____ Fans

c. The Speaker of the House of Commons was unable to obey the kings command because _____ he had a bad foot

Julius Caesar is famous for his telegram; I came, I saw, I conquered. He also wrote a book for beginners in Latin.

St. Bartholomew was massacred in 1492

By the Salic law no woman or descendant of a woman could occupy the throne.

The Puritans went to America for an asylum and found an insane asylum in the wilds of America.

The Indians pursued their warfare by hiding in the bushes and scalping them.

Queen Elizabeth was so fond of dresses that she was never seen without one.

Classic Collection

The revolting peasants were known as the beaujolais. They all sang the mayonnaise and went about shouting Liberty, Equaliaty and Maternity.

Queen Elizabeth had a difficult reign because Mary Queen of Scots was always hoovering in the background.

GEOGRAPHY

The Ouse flows horizontally past Hull after flowing vertically through York.

We did Canada and had to sing a song called "The Maypole Leaf for Ever."

Trees near farmhouses act as windbreaks. A fifty foot tree can break wind for over 150 yards.

The Arabs are anxious to make water in the desert areas.

The mountains between France and Spain are known as the Pyramids.

Japan has such a number of inhabitants that the island is slowly sinking.

Coca Cola is a West African crop.

Intensive cultivation means all the crops are grown inside.

Reindeer provide meat, milk, butter, cheese and eggs.

The Manchester Ship Canal is very important because before it was made all the ships were unloaded at Liverpool and sent by train to Manchester.

The Eskimo is a fisher and a hunter. When he catches a whale he takes it to his tent and his wife will cook it.

Groups of islands in the Pacific include the Philistines.

Longitude and latitude are very useful. Suppose a man is drowning he has only to shout out what latitude and longitude he is in and then we can find him.

Coral wreathes join India to Ceylon.

Yorkshire is in the rain shadow of the Pennines. This means that the rain is dryer.

CLASSIC COLLECTION

At the top of a volcano you see the creator smoking.

From the volcano came malt and larva.

The palaver flowed from the volcano.

Tourists float through Venice on gladiolas.

Farms on the Fens are very futile.

When we went to York we were shown parts of the minister that are not normally shown to the public.

SCHOOL VISITS

"Miss, Miss I did what you said; I asked the gardener if the flowers belonged to the primula family and he said that they belonged to the Town Council."

In the National Gallery in front of 'The Hay Wain.'
"Sir, somebody has copied that from one in my bedroom."

On seeing a Duke's robes in scarlet and ermine at a stately home
"Look that's where Father Christmas keeps his clothes"

We went to see Lake Windermere and it was lovely. We stood looking and drinking it all in until it was time to go.

When we had seen the nature reserve a man asked us to sign a partition to stop a road being built.

We went to the Cathedral and saw lots of carvings on the seats of holy people.

Before I set off for London my brother told me of some of the places we would see and so I was expectant. Now I'm even more expectant.

Before we went to the nature reserve we were told not to eat any berries because they can kill you. You should never touch the deadly lightshade.

In London we saw where the Queen lives. It is like a palace.

The guide told us that in the Fire of London the worst flaming place of all was St. Pauls and they had to build a new one.

Postcard

Dear Mummy and Daddy,

Sitting here drinking orange juice while the teachers have a giraffe of wine and wont give us any.

Love,

Adele.

We went to the safari park to see the loins and a bamboo sat on the bonnet of our car.

SCHOOL TRIPS

Dear Mother,

Please write soon even if it is only two or three pounds.

Love,

Clint

Dear Mother,

This skiing is brill. You can see the mountains touring above the clouds.

Jason

Dear Mam and Dad,

This postcard is of a windmill in Holland. They work by water power from the canals.

Teacher in charge

"Now listen carefully – you must all be back here ready to get on the coach at three o'clock precisely, and when I say three o'clock precisely I mean three o'clock precisely. I do not mean ten minutes past I mean ten minutes to."

Dear Mam and Dad,

Very nice here. Sleeping on an inferior sprung mattress.

Love

Bev.

We saw the farmer playing with the cows rudders and some milk came out.

After making the tea wash the teapot and stand upside down on the draining board.

HOME ECONOMICS

Slow cooking in a camisole is the best way to do cheap meat. It can be quite tasty if plenty of spies are used.

Having solved one problem by having double glazing you may have another – condescension.

Odd Spelling
MTATATIPI (Meat and Potato (Tatey) Pie)

Double glazing has been known to cause compensation.

Before you get married there is the exciting time when you are preparing your torso.

In a big class like this it is very difficult for every girl to fry at the same time.

If you are worried about using water from a well or stream then it should be boiled until it is putrified.

Moths do not eat much – they eat holes in coats.

To make the cake, take the dried fruit and butter and rub well into the floor.

Inside the chicken there is a blizzard.

When there are no fresh vegetables you can get canned.

Report
Cookery: Kim failed to defrost the food.

Be sure to buy a stove big enough to fit the entire family.

Then sprinkle the cake with desecrated coconut.

It is cheaper to cook at home because the cost of meals in cafes is exuberant and children can be vociferous eaters.

In our living room we have a 3p sweet.

In our class we invite people to lunch which we plan and cook. One day we had the Head for lunch. When we had roast beef the History mistress calved.

If you let the knife slip you can cut yourself severely in the kitchen.

We were taught manners such as never break your bread or roll in the soup.

It is cleaner if sliced meat is picked up with tongues.

When cleaning dresses care is needed if the lining is of man mad fivers.

Food should be kept clean and well away from flies and dirty incest.

Perishing foods must be watched carefully.

There are special diets for invalids and glutton free diets.

Nutrition was very good on the farm. They had milk from their own cows and honey from their own bee.

SCIENCE

A lot of atoms together are called monocles.

Graffitti
The science teacher's gone to heaven,
We won't see him no more,
For what he thought was H_2O
Was H_2SO_4!

Water boils in a Celcius thermometer at 100 degrees but boils at a much higher temperature in a Fahrenheit one.

The Chiltern Hundreds can be seen in their thousands in cheese under a microscope.

Science Master to give Talk on Moon

Of the Planets, Venus, Juniper and perhaps the earth was known to ancient man.

An inclined plane is a plane that inclines and if the experiment is successful then the result is inevitable.

A Chemistry experiment with a burette is described.
We observe the bottom of the brunette until we see the drops of water fall.

The Lord of Gravity was created when Newton dropped an apple from the Leaning Tower of Pisa.

Question: How would you measure the height of a tall building using an aneroid barometer?

Answer: I would lower the barometer from the top on the end of a piece of string and then measure the string.

IT'S A SCIENTIFIC FACT

Light goes through your spectacles and is focused on the rectum.

There are three kinds of levers, Christmas, Easter and Summer but soon there might be only two kinds of levers.

There are three icicles in the inner ear. They are the hammer, the axle and the spanner.

When steam turns back into water it is by conversation.

Health and safety are important in a laboratory. Some poisons are so strong that one drop on a dog's tongue will kill a strong man.

When you are watching a solar eclipse never look at the sun. It is possible to use smoked glass to see the eclipse but care is needed and you must not stand too close.

Radiation means what comes out of an electric fire and the interviewing medium is not heated.

The difference between air and water is that air can be made humid and water cannot be made any more humid.

The gas that is given off is very harmful to human beings and the following experiment should therefore only be performed by a teacher.

If sixty feet of an iceberg is above water the rest of it is below.

> Cassidy, the soccer captain, played well and dominated the game. A brilliant run defeated three opponents and a faultless pass was made to Williams, who, under pressure, lost his head and kicked it over the bar.
>
> Finally Williams scored from a difficult angel

Report on the school football match

PHYSICAL EDUCATION

Reports

Jane is a keen participant in all games and she is shaping up very nicely. Her form is very impressive for a girl of sixteen.

You will note that Mark has gained a considerable amount around the waist. He is always missing games and it has been observed that he will neither read nor learn but only inwardly digest.

The Primary School class doing PE in the playground in winter.

"Please Miss it's cold because somebody's left the gate open."

The Headmaster of a church school was very keen on football and used to encourage his team by screaming from the touchline, "Come on, come on St. Marks use your wings!"

Letter to school
Dear Sir,

Margaret can't have Jim this week. She had Jim last week and she could hardly move and she's still a bit sore.

Yours sincerely,

Mrs. T.

Riddle
What has 22 legs and goes around screaming?

The School Hockey Team

Dear Gym Teacher,

Will you please excuse John from P.E. because of his eyes as he can't see without them and he can't wear them because he has smashed them twice.

Yours truly,

Mrs. Lord.

P.E. Teacher: "Jack your feet are filthy."

Jack: "Yes Sir."

P.E. Teacher: "Have you been in bed with them like that?"

Jack: "Yes Sir."

P.E. Teacher: "I shudder to think what the bedclothes are like."

Jack: "They're O.K. I keep my socks on in bed."

"Why am I always put in the second team?" asked Tom.

P.E. Teacher, "Because we haven't got a third team."

| Dead Teacher Noted
Among Sportsmen |

No boy must swim in any water not passed by the Headmaster.

HEALTH AND FIRST AID

Foreigners bodies can be dangerous if they get into the eye.

The vines go round the body and end up at the heart which is comical in shape.

Look at the eyes and see if the pupils are diluted.

The doctor must be called if someone has got selfish poisoning and you must hope that he arrives on time.

Carpets and rugs should be kept clean because babies crawl on them so beat them and shampoo them.

Skin is what holds us together and without it we would fall apart.

Sewage has been around for a long time. It was known to the Romans and the Normans knew about it too.

There was a lot of TB at one time but it is not so popular now.

After the food has been in the stomach it then is waste and has to pass out of the body through the rectory.

Waist disposal is very important.

SEX EDUCATION

The law was changed so that things were alright with scented adults.

When they take the pill ladies make eggs without yolks.

The uterus in women is hidden by the pelvic gurgle.

Sexually transmitted diseases, such as unwanted pregnancy should be avoided.

Now girls I have explained the various methods of contraception but I must tell you that I have not personal experience of them all but if you wish to know more I can put you in touch with the appropriate body.

When you are expecting you should always attend the anti-naval clinic.

Couples should practise family planning because practise makes perfect.

Five Year Old: "Mrs. Kay had twins — that's two babies; You buy one and get one free."

RELIGIOUS EDUCATION

False Doctrine is when the doctor gives you the wrong sort of medicine.

Fast Days were when they tried to eat in a hurry.

CLASSIC

Elisha was a holy man who went on a cruise with a widow. He had a bear and children mocked him and he said if you mock me I will set my bear on you and it will eat you up. And they did and he did and it did.

Jesus was betrayed by Judas Asparagus

Letter

To the Teacher of Religious? Education

Dear Sir,

I am told by a choirboy that you have been telling them about religions other than Christianity. I am a church-warden – isn't this a scandal?

Yours faithfully,

T.H.L.

After telling my class the Easter story one eight year old boy, who had been listening with great attention said,

"Isn't that shocking Miss?"

"Isn't what shocking Paul?" I replied.

"That Judas should sell Jesus for thirty pieces of silver."

"It certainly is," I agreed, delighted that the story had such a profound effect.

"Yes," he continued, "he could have got at least a hundred."

You find priests in the Bible and in some churches where they burn insects.

Joseph had a goat of many colours.

CLASSIC TRIO

Noah's wife was Joan of Arc

Solomon had many wives and cucumbers.

Samson in the theatre brought down the house.

* * *

A primate is the husband of a lady Prime Minister like Denis Thatcher.

The Bishop came to the convent and in a short service made one of the sisters into a Mother.

The bishop blessed me and I hadn't sneezed.

When the probable son came back home everybody was very pleased except the fatted calf.

To do a baptism you need water and a baby.

When the Jews left Egypt they wandered in the dessert.

CLASSIC

The most frequently submitted classic howler with a lesser known addition.

Salome danced naked in front of Harrods.

She wore very few clothes and took off more than she had put on.

One version of Pentecost.

So the disciples decided to have a party and they were all filled with the holy spirits.

Another version.

. . . and they was all seated in an upper room and suddenly something came through and they all felt hot.

The Good Samaritan

"Why did the priest and Levi pass by on the other side?"

"Because they would have seen that the man had already been robbed."

Write what you know of the Last Supper

I was away for the Last Supper – I had mumps.

A man who reads the Bible from cover to cover and keeps on doing it is called a bibliomaniac.

Tell, in your own words, the story of a Parable.

This man went out to sew seeds. Some of these seeds fell on nice ground and some fell on stones. Which only goes to show that you have to watch what you are doing when you are sewing seeds.

Faith is believing what you know is not true.

"And then children," said the vicar, "we will see the footprints of the Almighty, welcoming us with both arms."

Conscience is a small voice inside us and is sometimes called an invoice.

Moses gave his people a massage.

If David had a fault it was a slight tendency to adultery.

Mesopotamia was the cradle of fertilisation.

The Vatican Council proclaimed the inflammability of the Pope.

A Headmaster writes;

Disgusted with the daily mumbling of the Lord's Prayer I instructed the whole school to spend the first period writing out the words from memory. The school buzzed like a swarm of bees as children recited the words to themselves phrase by phrase. Few got it right. Odd phrases like "Halliwell be thy name" appeared – Halliwell is a suburb of Bolton. I mentioned the exercise to the Head of a neighbouring Catholic school who decided to repeat the experiment. He rang me later to report a version of "Hail Mary"

Hail Mary, full of grace, the Lord is with thee,
Blessed art thou a monk's women.

Vicar Upset By School Sex Position

The vicar with the ten year olds

Vicar: "Would any boy or girl like to ask me a question?"

Jack: "Please vicar you know that bit in the Bible when the angels went up and down the ladder?"

Vicar: "Of course."

Jack: "Well vicar, why did they not use their wings?"

Vicar: "Would any boy or girl like to answer that question?"

Molly, the daughter of a pigeon fancier,

'Perhaps they were moulting."

A child's view of Hymn Boards.

When we went into the church there were some numbers on a board and I worked it out that they didn't add up right.

Teacher: ". . . and God made winged creatures."

Voice: "Aeroplanes, Miss?"

The teacher was describing the plight of the blind man in the Bible story and was reminded of one handicap which she had not mentioned by a voice exclaiming: "He wouldn't be able to see his pools coupon!"

An Indian sinner will be prepared by 5th form girls to raise money.

HUMAN BIOLOGY

The circulation of the blood in the body was started by Harvey. He noticed that blood went in vines around the body.

After the milk teeth the teeth that come through are permanent but not as permanent as false teeth.

The ducks from the kidneys make their way to the bladder.

When people breathe in they inspire and when they breathe out they expire.

Dear Miss,

     I do not want our Bridget learning that Human Biology especially below the waist as it upsets her and puts her off her food.

     Thank you,

     Mrs. Cook.

Germans are very small and there can be thousands of them in one drop of dirty water.

Dear Mr. Evans, (BIOLOGY)

     Do you think I should have my baby humanised against hooping cough? Please tell Harry the answer and oblige.

     Harrys Mother.

MUSIC

Teacher: "On Wednesday afternoon, after school I shall be taking an extra music class. Is there anyone here who would like to learn to play a recorder?"

"I can already play a recorder," scoffed one seven year boy, "why I can even play a music centre."

I was going to play the piano in the school concert but lost my courage at the last minuet.

Teacher: "Ralph. What is the time signature?"

Ralph: "It's quarter to twelve, Miss."

An impromtu vote of thanks to the Liverpool Philharmonic Orchestra after a concert for schools. A Headmaster speaks . . .

"The orchestra will be interested to know that half of the children in the audience had a days holiday today, but instead of enjoying themselves they came here to listen to you."

Beethoven wrote two symphonies, the Fifth which is very nice, and the Ninth.

A famous musician in Manchester was the conductor of the Hallé orchestra, Sir John B. Rolli.

Beethoven had an expectant mother but an indifferent father.

REPORT

Music: The pieces Barbara chose to play were commendably short.

From a Junior

"I would like to be in a Salvation Army Band and play the tangerine."

I would like to be good at music and play the goitre like Paul McCartney.

On the Last Night of the Proms they all get excited and sing Ruby Tanyer.

Head: "I didn't know we had a music lesson at this time."

Secretary: "We don't – that's the cleaner dusting the piano.

A fugue is when all the windows are shut in a crowded room with everybody smoking.

Teacher: "What's that you are reading Michael?"

Michael: "It's my music Miss."

He handed over a piece of paper with the letters bbsssbb

"Music Michael?"

"Yes Miss, for my mouth organ Blow, Blow, Suck, Suck, Suck."

> The Headmaster said that student flies would not be opened for inspection. "They contain items of a personal nature which should not be revealed casually," he said,

SCHOOL REPORTS

Although some drink deeply at the fountain of knowledge I regret that Colin simply gargles.

Diana has been very active in many fields around the school.

Tony sets himself very low standards which he then fails to achieve.

He is so weak at Geography that it is amazing that he finds his way to school.

Christmas Term. Headmaster's Comment.

Quite one of the worst reports I have ever read showing the results of truancy, idleness and bad behaviour. He must improve.

Easter Term.

Very bad indeed – a great improvement

* * *

Formteacher's Comment:

Ruth talks far too much

Parent's Comment:

You should hear her mother.

* * *

Jane learns from her mistakes but she, unfortunately, remembers to repeat them.

Geography   E
History   E
English   E
Maths   E
Art   E

Comments: Very consistent work

Comment on the report of a boy suspected of cheating and writing his own absence notes.

Forging steadily ahead.

Adrian tends to confuse things. He describes it as putting the horse before the cart.

He says he will go down in history. He will also go down in English and Geography.

Boy Suspended by Head

"Parents Evening is now over — will you please leave the Hall as the caretaker and I are very anxious to get to bed."

THE CARETAKER HAS HIS SAY . . .

Caretaker: "I can write my name in the dust on this desk."

Cleaner: "Isn't education a fine thing."

"You shouldn't use that telephone for personal calls. You should use the chaos in the village."

"The teachers here put weight on because it's a sedimentary occupation."

"The teachers are full of airs and graces; we have holidays but they have vaccinations."

"I told them not to adopt that platitute with me."

"I'll just have this sandwich to keep the wood from the door."

"I am not putting my head in the lion's noose for anybody."

"They have sent a heavy shovel that will castrate my back."

"The man from local radio is here, the reporter is coming – we can't get on with our work with all the mediocre here."

"The new brushes are well below my expectorations."

"I can't get that writing off the wall. They have used an indelicate pen."

NOTICE

If the person who removed the stepladders from my storeroom does not return them further steps will be taken.

71

SCHOOL MEALS

The names children give to school food

Bakewell Tart: bakelite tart

Beefburgers: shoe soles

Cottage Pie: condemned by the Council

Beans on Toast: skinheads on a raft

Spaghetti: worms in gravy, shoelaces.

Cauliflower: brains

Fish in White sauce: Whale and whitewash

Rice pudding and jam: a road accident

Ravioli: soggy pillows

Sago: frogs spawn

Currant Pie: flies cemetery

Canteen Supervisor, writing the menu: "How do you spell Blancmange?"

Assistant: "B – L – O – M – M, no B – L – U – M no that's not right either — better give them rice."

Wayne (aged six) "What does vanilla taste like?;;

Harry (aged seven) "Everybody knows that vanilla is the opposite of chocolate."

Headmistress: "I've been thinking that with all this trend towards healthier eating we should think of having vegetarian dishes."

Canteen Supervisor: "I once worked in a vegetarian place and we had to put artificial flowers on the table. If we used real ones they ate them!"

AROUND THE PRIMARY SCHOOL

"Today," said the teachers, "we're going to study graphs. Does anyone know what a graph is?"

"I do," responded a small child, anxious to air her knowledge.

"It's an animal with a very long neck."

The vicar asked the class how many boys and girls would like to go to Heaven. Only one little girl kept her hand down. When the vicar asked her why she replied. "Me mum said I had to go straight home."

"Please Vicar, do cats go to Heaven because our next door neighbours cat has been put to sleep?"

"It may be in Heaven."

"But, Vicar, will God know that it likes blue label catfood best?"

The Headmistress interviews ...

An immigrant mother who has just moved into the area.

"Is your son a natural born citizen of this country?"

"No, he was born by Caesarean birth."

"I'm sorry I meant was he born here."

"No he was born when we lived in London."

"Oh yes — how old was he when he was born?"

The mother of eight children.

"How on earth do you cope with eight children?"

"Well when I had one baby she occupied every minute I had. What more time can eight babies take?"

AROUND THE HIGH SCHOOL

Irate teacher

"Smith — you are not fit to be in this room!

I think that you are a disgrace to your family and to the school. You are not fit to mix with decent people — go to the Headmaster at once."

In the typing class.

"This is much better Jenny, only six mistakes so far."

"Oh good, Miss."

"Now we'll look at the second sentence."

In the School Library.

"Please Miss, I want to stop being the Library Prefect as I'm not sleeping at night and my mother thinks it's the responsibility."

Graffiti

FAITH CAN MOVE MOUNTAINS. SHE'S A BIG GIRL!

SUPPORT HIRE EDUCATION!

The new teacher

"Good morning — I am your new English Teacher and my name is Evans. E — V – A – N – S. E for epistemology, V for vignette, A for ascidium, N for nenuphar, and S for siriasis.

The Geography teacher uses the video

"Now, from the Canadian side, you see the magnificent Niagara Falls, with millions of gallons of water falling over and eroding . . . and if you would stop talking for a moment you would hear the incredible roar."

Discussing homework

"No Ruth — entrechat does not mean a cat door."

"The French for eggs is not pommes de poule."

"Hors d'oeuvre does not mean out of work and Salle à manger does not mean sales manager."

"Habeus Corpus has nothing to do with the Plague and does not, repeat not, mean 'Bring out your dead."

"Harry you have written that the Franciscans were founded by St. Francis of the Sea Sick in Italy."

Notice

THESE HOOKS ARE FOR TEACHERS ONLY

to which someone added

THEY CAN ALSO BE USED FOR COATS !

"Who's your form master this year?"

"Young Stinks."

"The new chemistry master?"

"No he takes History – he has this problem with his feet."

CHRISTMAS AT SCHOOL

Christmas at School

From an essay.

On Christmas Eve everybody in the family goes to Midnight Maths. The gifts of the Three Wise Men were gold and francs.

THE NATIVITY PLAY

Garbled lines

Thus spake the sherrif and forthwith appeared a shining throng.

Hail, said the angel, Hail thou that art highly flavoured.

"Merry Christmas to you all," said the teacher, "and don't stuff yourselves silly."

"Same to you Miss," chorused the class.

"Please Miss, what does Father Christmas give his mother?"

The Headmistress saw the two children who were rehearsing the parts of Mary and Joseph pinch each other, then slaps were exchanged and a fight began. She separated them and explained that in the play they were acting the parts of a married couple who were kind and loving. Ten minutes later they were fighting again.

"Why?" asked the Headmistress.

"Please Miss. he tried to kiss me!"

"Please Miss," said Joseph, "she is my wife."

BREAKING UP

No more pencils, no more books,
No more teacher's dirty looks!

A mournful boy at the end of his first year at school said to the
Reception Class Teacher.
'Oh, Mrs. Webster, isn't it a pity that you're not clever enough to
teach us next year.'